IRIS Folding for the Winter

Maruscha Gaasenbeek
Tine Beauveser

FORTE PUBLISHERS

Contents

Original title: *Irisvouwen in wintersfeer*

Second printing August 2002
ISBN 90 5877 201 2

This is a publication from
Forte Publishers BV
Boothstraat 1c
3512 BT Utrecht
The Netherlands

For more information about the creative books available from Forte Uitgevers:
www.hobby-party.com

Publisher: Marianne Perlot
Editor: Hanny Vlaar
Photography and digital image editing: Fotografie Gerhard Witteveen, Apeldoorn, the Netherlands
Cover and inner design: Studio Herman Bade BV, Baarn, the Netherlands

Preface

Welcome to IRIS folding, the easy folding technique with fantastic results. All the cards in **IRIS Folding for the Winter** are filled with strips cut from the inside of envelopes. Therefore, collect as many envelopes as you can. Swap them with others and sort them into different colours. We have managed to collect almost 400 different colours and patterns! In this book, envelope paper has also been used as a intermediate sheet for the cards. Multifunctional mini stickers, with or without a shiny border, are special decorations. And the narrow strips of holographic paper give the Christmas cards a festive look.

Your own, always varying, choice of paper and finishing material makes every card unique and creative.

We wish you lots of enjoyment with all the new patterns!

Maruscha Tine

Thanks to: Alma and Hanny for the enjoyable cooperation, and especially to Marianne for her stimulating enthusiasm, creative advice and warm, personal attention.

Techniques

The starting point for IRIS folding is the pattern. Cut the outer shape of the pattern out of the card and then fill the hole from the outside to the inside with folded strips of used envelopes. You work at the back of your card, so that you work in fact on a mirror image. When you have finished, you stick the card onto another card. For a rectangular pattern, select four different envelopes where the patterns and colours combine and contrast each other nicely.
Cut all the envelopes into strips in the same way, for example, from left to right. Depending on the pattern, you will need between four and eight strips. The width of the strips also depends on the pattern and is stated for each card.
First, you need to fold an edge of the strips over and sort them into each different type of envelope. Next, you cover each section in turn by following the numbers (1, 2, 3, 4, 5, etc.), so that you rotate the design. Lay the strips with the fold facing towards the middle of the pattern and then stick them on the left-hand and right-hand sides of the card using adhesive tape. Finally, use an attractive piece of deco tape to cover the hole in the middle. Avoid colour differences by using only one envelope for the same design.

The basic rectangle

(see card 1 in chapter 1)

The most important thing is to start with the basic rectangle, because from this, you will learn the unique folding and sticking technique needed for all the patterns. You will notice that you quickly get used to the technique of IRIS folding.

Preparation

1. Lay a white card (13.8 x 9.5 cm) down with the back facing towards you.
2. Draw around the circumference of the rectangle on the card and cut it out.
3. Stick a copy of the basic rectangle given in this book (pattern 1) on your cutting mat using adhesive tape.
4. Place the card with the hole on the pattern (you should be looking at the back of the card) and only stick the left-hand side of the card to your cutting mat using masking tape.
5. Choose four envelopes with different patterns. Four different red, blue and grey envelopes have been used for the card shown on page 9 in the top left-hand corner.
6. Cut 2.5 cm *wide* strips from these envelopes and make separate piles of colour A, colour B, colour C and colour D.
7. For each strip, fold a border (approximately

1. The inside of some of the more than four hundred different envelopes.

2. Cut the rectangle out of the back of a single card. Cut the envelopes into strips and fold an edge of the strips over.

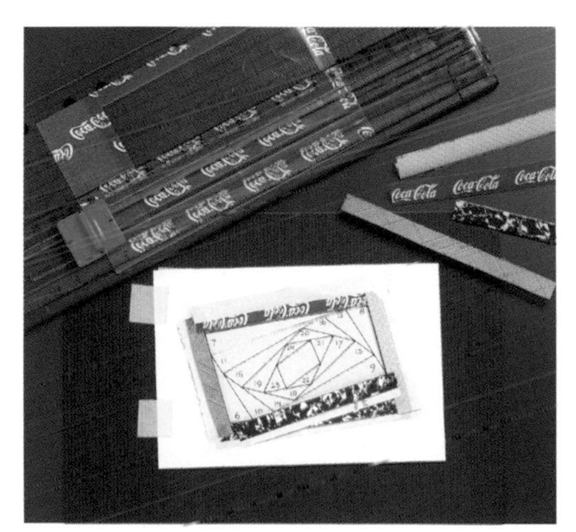

3. Stick the pattern to your cutting mat and place the card on top of it. Place the strips exactly against the line and stick down the left-hand and right-hand sides using adhesive tape.

4. Fold the card open from time to time to see whether the patterns continue nicely.

7 mm) along its entire length with the *nice side facing outwards*.

IRIS folding

8. Take a folded strip of colour A and place this over section 1, exactly against the line of the pattern with the folded side facing towards the middle. Allow 0.5 cm to stick out on the left-hand and right-hand sides and cut the rest off. By doing so, the strip will also slightly stick out over the edge of the pattern at the bottom, so that section 1 is totally covered.
9. Stick the strip to the card on the left-hand and right-hand sides using a small piece of adhesive tape, but remain 0.5 cm from the edge of the card.
10. Take a strip of colour B and place it on section 2 of the pattern. Also tape this to the left-hand and right-hand sides of the card.
11. Take a strip of colour C. Place this on section 3 and stick it into place.
12. Take a strip of colour D. Place this on section 4 and stick it into place.
13. Start again with colour A on section 5, colour B on section 6, colour C on section 7 and colour D on section 8. The strips on sections 1, 5, 9, 13, 17 and 21 of this pattern are all of colour A. The strips on sections 2, 6, 10, 14, 18 and 22 are all of colour B. The strips on sections 3, 7, 11, 15, 19 and 23 are all of colour C. The strips on sections 4, 8, 12, 16, 20 and 24 are all of colour D.

Finishing

After section 24, carefully remove the card. Stick a piece of holographic paper in the middle on the back of the card. You can use punches, figure scissors, embossing stencils, etc. to add extra finishing touches to the card. Stick small pieces of double-sided adhesive tape along the edges. Remove the protective layer from the tape and fix your design on a double card. Do not use glue, because all the paper strips place pressure on the card.

Making glitter borders

Fold a narrow border around strips of holographic paper and add these to the strips of envelope paper. First, stick a strip of envelope paper to the card against the section's dotted line. Place a strip of holographic paper on the strip of envelope paper with the fold against the section's solid line and stick it in place. Glitter strips are, therefore, added to the patterns which have dotted lines.

Embossing

To emboss, place the stencil on the good side of the card and stick it in place using masking tape. Place the card (with the stencil) upside-down on a light box. Carefully push the paper through the stencil's opening using the embossing pen. You only have to push along the edges to raise the entire image.

Materials

To make the cards:

- ❏ *Card: Canson Mi-Teintes (C), Artoz (A) en Papicolor (P)*
- ❏ *IRIS folding text stickers*
- ❏ *Vellum*
- ❏ *Bank notes*
- ❏ *Cutting knife*
- ❏ *Cutting mat*
- ❏ *Ruler with a metal cutting edge (Securit)*
- ❏ *Adhesive tape*
- ❏ *Double-sided adhesive tape*
- ❏ *Masking tape*
- ❏ *Split pins*
- ❏ *Various punches (TomTas, Make me!, Media)*
- ❏ *Multi-corner punch (Reuser)*
- ❏ *Punch with exchangeable shapes (TomTas)*
- ❏ *Hole punch*
- ❏ *Scissors and silhouette scissors*
- ❏ *Corner scissors (Fiskars)*
- ❏ *Photo glue*
- ❏ *Ridge master*
- ❏ *Embossing pen*
- ❏ *Various embossing stencils (Avec, Linda Design, Make Me!)*
- ❏ *Light box*

IRIS folding

- ❏ *Strips of used envelopes*

The middle of the card

- ❏ *Deco tape*
- ❏ *Holographic paper*
- ❏ *Origami paper*

The patterns:

Full-size examples of all the patterns are given in this book. Copy them using a light box or use the A4-size, transparent, plastic IRIS folding-and-drawing template, which has six different patterns. The shapes are usually easy to cut out of the card. Special, punched cards are available for the pear, the coffee pot, the icicle and the Christmas tree.

Rectangles

Boxes with presents and games for cosy, long winter evenings.

This model can be used both in portrait and landscape format. For all the cards, follow the instructions given for the basic rectangle (see Techniques).

Card 1 basic rectangle

Card: bright red C506 (10.5 x 29.7 cm) and white (9.5 x 13.8 cm) • Pattern 1 • 2.5 cm wide strips from 4 different red, grey and blue envelopes • Silver holographic paper

Card 2

Card: white (14.8 x 21 cm and 12.8 x 8.5 cm) • Pattern 1 • 2.5 cm wide strips from 4 different blue envelopes • Blue envelope paper (14 x 9.2 cm) • Text sticker • Silver holographic paper • Celestial corner scissors

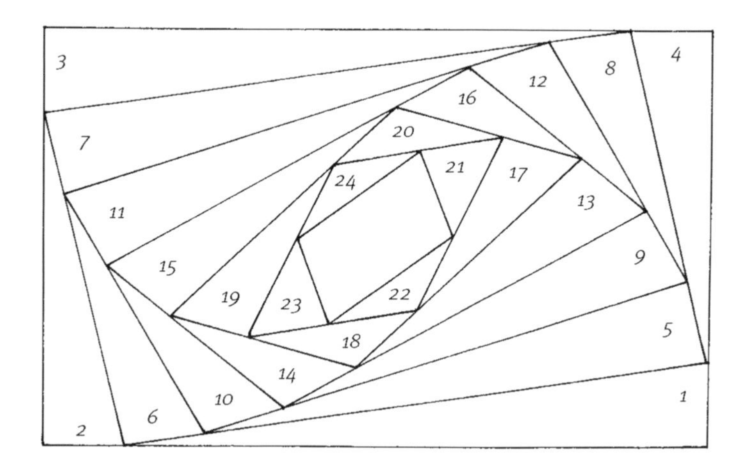

Pattern 1

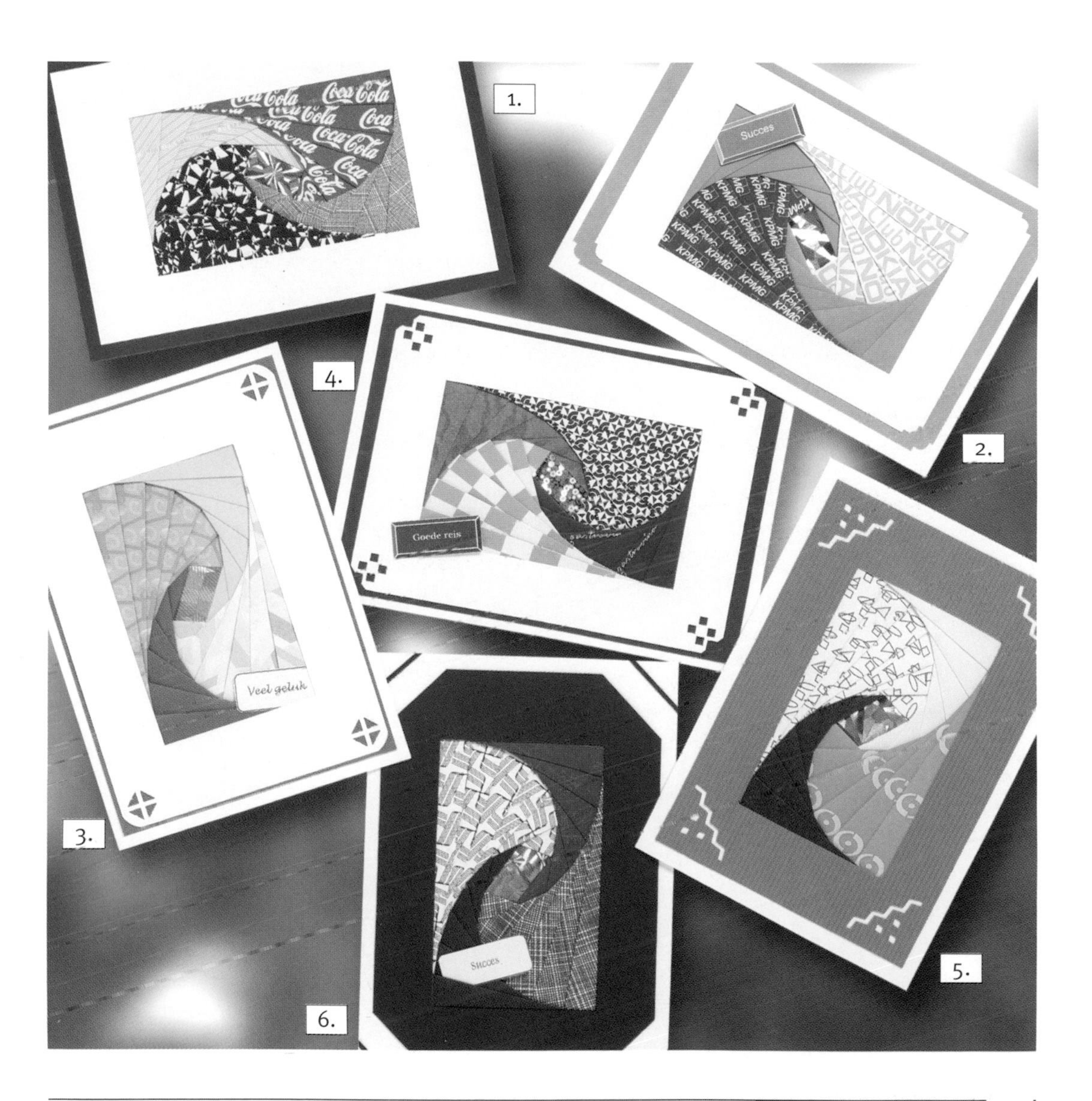
1.
Succes
2.
4.
Goede reis
Veel geluk
3.
Succes
5.
6.

Cut off all the corners of the small white card and the piece of envelope paper using the corner scissors. After the IRIS folding, stick the text sticker on the card.

Card 3

Card: white (14.8 x 21 cm and 13.8 x 9.6 cm) • Pattern 1 • 2.5 cm wide strips from 4 different yellow/grey-green envelopes • Grey-green envelope paper (14.1 x 9.9 cm) • Text sticker • Silver holographic paper • Multi-corner punch

Punch out the corners of the small white card.

Card 4

Card: white (14.8 x 21 cm and 13 x 9.5 cm) • Pattern 1 • 2.5 cm wide strips from 4 different purple envelopes • Purple envelope paper (14 x 9.9 cm) • Text sticker • Gold deco tape • Multi-corner punch

Punch out the corners of the small white card.

Card 5

Card: white (14.8 x 21 cm) and grey-green (13.8 x 9.5 cm) • Pattern 1 • 2.5 cm wide strips of 4 white, yellow, grey-green and blue envelopes • Silver holographic paper • Diamond corner punch

Punch out the corners of the grey-green card.

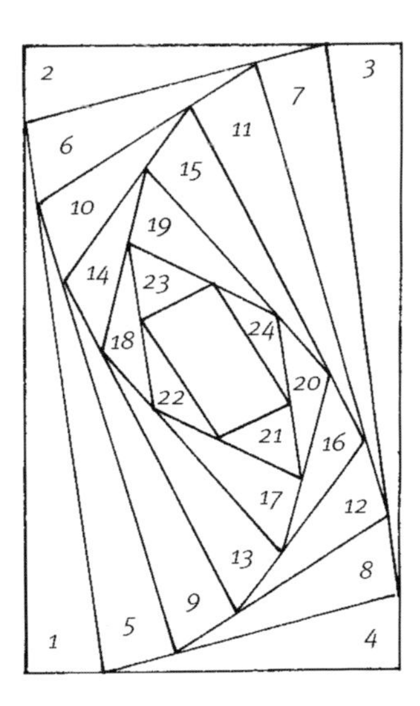

Pattern 2

Card 6

Card: white (14.8 x 21 cm) and red (13.7 x 9.5 cm) • 0.2 cm wide strips of red card • Pattern 1 • 2.5 cm wide strips from 4 different envelopes • Text sticker • Silver holographic paper

Cut the corners of the red card at an angle. Stick the strips of red card exactly between the slanting line and the corners of the double card.

Playing with rectangles

Lively rectangles for creative enthusiasts and a gift envelope to hold a surprise.

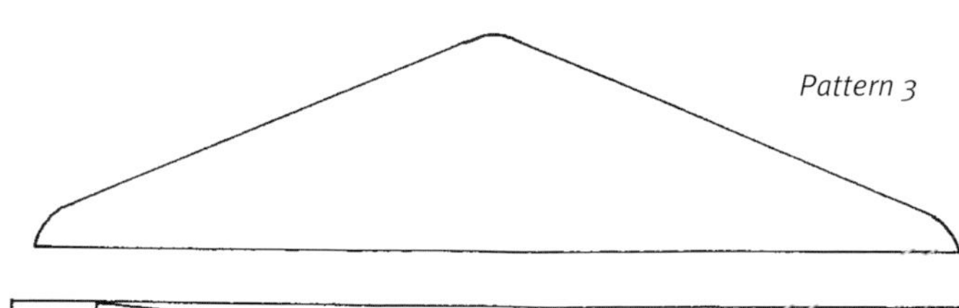

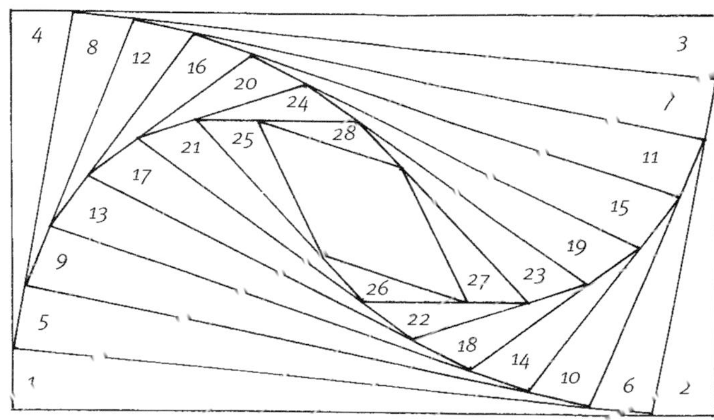

The gift envelopes are made according to the description given for card 3.

Card on page 1

Card: rusty-brown C504 (14.8 x 21 cm) and shell white C112 (13.8 x 9.5 cm) • Pattern 2 • 2 cm wide strips from 4 different brown/orange envelopes • Copper deco tape

Cut the rectangles with an overlap of 0.8 cm out of the white card. Fill sections 1, 2 and 3 in the normal way. Fold a connecting strip along the two sides over the entire length to a width of 0.8 cm to cover section 4 of both rectangles. Carry on with the IRIS folding (section 5, 6, 7 etc.). Section 4 of the second rectangle has already been filled and, therefore, after section 3, carry on with sections 5, 6, etc.

Card 1

Card: lilac C104 (14.8 x 21 cm) and cornflower blue P05 (9.7 x 14 cm) • Pattern 2 • 2 cm wide strips from 4 different blue envelopes • Silver deco tape

Cut the small rectangle twice out of the blue

card. Next, cut off two opposite corners 2 cm from the point of the corner. Finish the card as described in the basic techniques.

Card 2

Card: cornflower blue P05 (14.8 x 21 cm) and lilac C104 (13.8 x 9.5 cm) • Pattern 2 • 2 cm wide strips from 4 different blue envelopes • Text sticker • Silver holographic paper

Place two copies of pattern 2 upside down next to each other so that section 1 of both rectangles touch each other. Fold one strip of envelope paper along the two sides over the entire length to a width of 0.7 cm and stick that strip over section 1 of both rectangles.

Card 3

Card: lavender blue C150 (14.8 x 21 cm) and white C335 (14.2 x 9.9 cm) • Pattern 3 • 2 cm wide strips from 4 different lilac and blue envelopes • € 5 • Silver holographic paper • Geometric embossing stencil • Congratulations embossing stencil

Emboss borders in three corners and emboss the text in the fourth corner. Only cut the rectangle out of the white card. Cut the flap out of envelope paper and stick it 0.5 cm above the rectangle. Cut the opening for the € 5 note according to the dotted line.

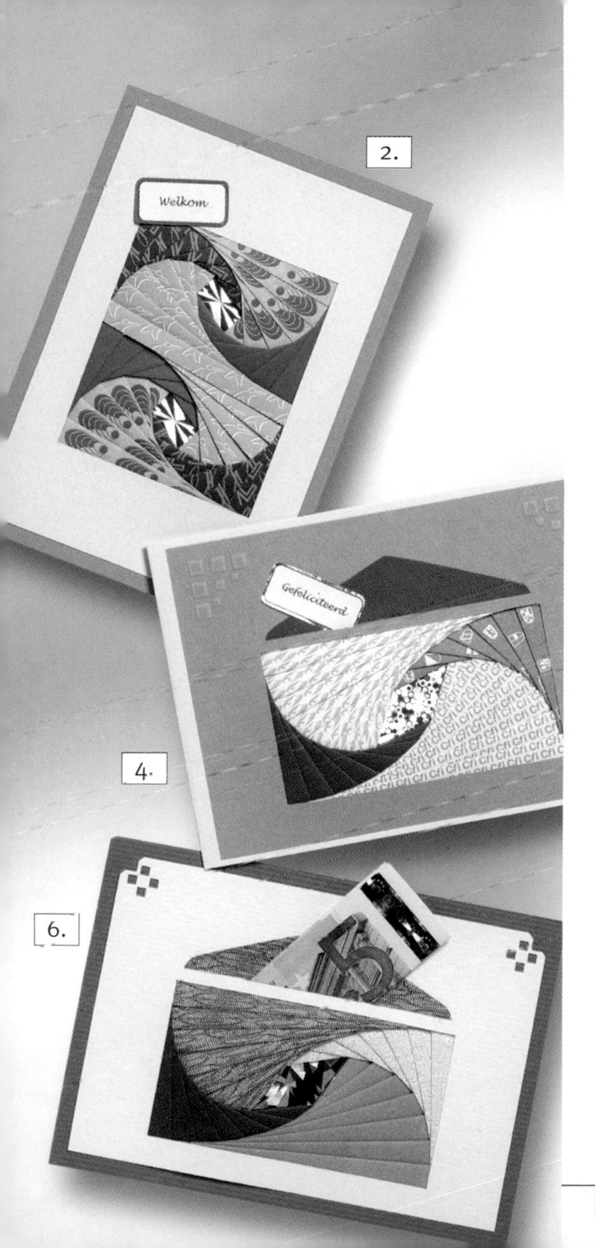

Card 4

Card: lilac C104 (10.5 x 29.7 cm) and pink C352 (10 x 13.8 cm) • Pattern 3 • 2 cm wide strips from 4 different grey and purple/red envelopes • Text sticker • Silver deco tape • Geometric embossing stencil

Emboss the top corners of the pink card.

Card 5

Card: cornflower blue P05 (10.5 x 29.7 cm) and pale blue C102 (14.3 x 10 cm) • Pattern 3 • 2 cm wide strips from 4 different envelopes • € 10 • Silver holographic paper • Multi-corner punch

Punch out two corners.

Card 6

Card: grey-green (10.5 x 29.7 cm) and pale yellow (9.5 x 13.8 cm) • Pattern 3 • 2 cm wide strips from 4 different grey/green envelopes • € 5 • Silver holographic paper • Multi-corner punch

Punch out the top corners of the yellow card.

Big and small leaves

Autumn, the time of falling leaves.

The big leaf is made according to the description given for card 1. The small leaf is made according to the description given for card 4.

Card 1

Card: sand C340 (14.8 x 21 cm) and dark blue A417 (13. X 9.5 cm) • Pattern 4 • 2 cm wide strips from 5 different brown envelopes • Gold holographic paper • Exchangeable ivy punch shape

Only cut out the leaf. After the IRIS folding, cut the stem out of envelope paper. Stick the stem and the leaves on the card.

Card 2

Card: chestnut brown C501 (14.8 x 21 cm), almond green C480 (13 x 9.5 cm) and gold (14.1 x 10.2 cm) • Pattern 4 • 2 cm wide strips from 5 different brown and green envelopes • Brown envelope paper (13.3 x 9.8 cm) • Text sticker • Gold holographic paper • Lily corner punch

Punch out the top corners of the green card. Tie the sticker to the stem using a thread.

Card 3

Card: white C335 (14.8 x 21 cm) and beige A241 (14 x 9 cm) • Pattern 4 • 2 cm wide strips from 5

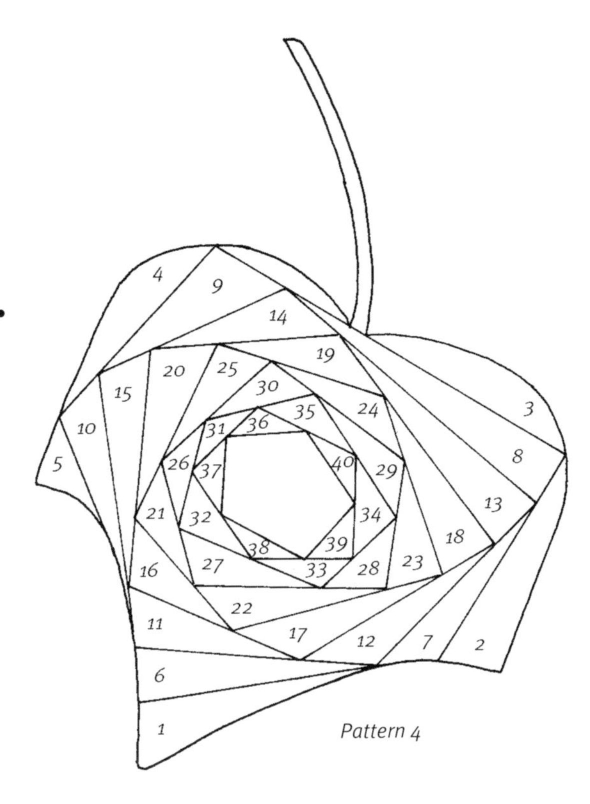

Pattern 4

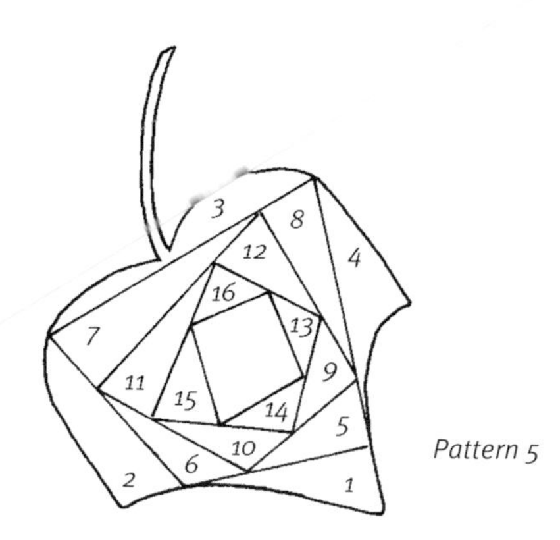

Pattern 5

different envelopes in various colours • Dark red envelope paper (14.4 x 9.4 cm) • Text sticker • Gold holographic paper • Victorian embossing stencil

Emboss the top and bottom of the beige card.

Card 4

Card: dark green (14.8 x 21 cm) and white C335 (8.2 x 7.6 cm and 5.5 x 5 cm) • Pattern 5 • 2 cm wide strips from 4 different red, beige and green envelopes • Green envelope paper (5.8 x 5.3 cm) • Vellum with a leaf pattern (14.8 x 21 cm) and a 7 x 6.5 cm window • Gold holographic paper

Cut the leaf out of the smallest card and fill the hole with strips. Stick all the cards onto each other. Fold the vellum around the card and indicate where to cut using a pencil. Remove the sheet, fold the vellum open and cut out the window. Stick a strip of double-sided adhesive tape on the back of the card along the line of the fold and stick the vellum to the card.

Card 5

Card: cornflower blue A425 (14.8 x 21 cm), silver (7.7 x 6.5 cm) and white C335 (6.7 x 5.5 cm) • Pattern 5 • 2 cm wide strips from 4 different purple envelopes • Vellum with a leaf pattern (14.8 x 21 cm) and a 7.3 x 6 cm window • Text sticker • Silver holographic paper

Card 6

Card: apple green C475 (14.8 x 21 cm), gold (7.7 x 6.5 cm) and white C335 (6.7 x 5.5 cm) • Pattern 5 • 2 cm wide strips from 4 different green envelopes • Vellum with a leaf pattern (14.8 x 21 cm) and a 7.1 x 6 cm window • Gold deco tape

1.
2.
Veel liefs
3.
Beterschap
4.
5.
6.

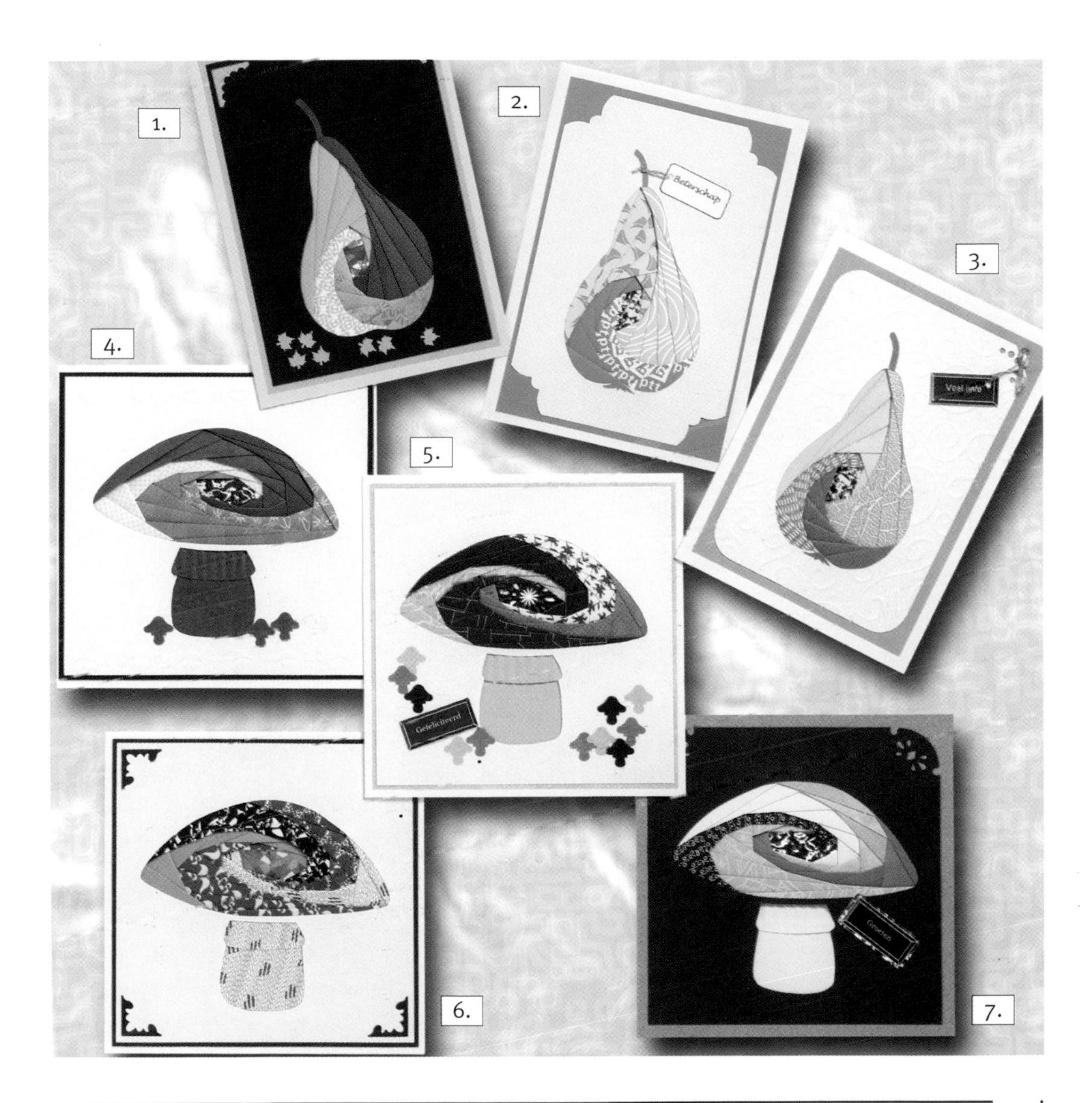
1.
2.
Beterschap
3.
4.
5.
Gefeliciteerd
6.
Groeten
7.

Pears and mushrooms

Autumn fruit.

The pears are made according to the description given for card 1.
The mushrooms are made according to the description given for card 4. Pattern 6 is given on page 32.

Card 1

Card: pearl grey C120 (14.8 x 21 cm) and wine red C503 (13.3 x 9 cm) • Pattern 6 • 2 cm wide strips from 4 different lilac, red and aubergine envelopes • Pink envelope paper (13.8 x 9.6 cm) • Silver holographic paper • Flower corner punch • Leaf mini punch

Punch out the top corners. Cut out the pear. Cut the stem out off envelope paper. Punch out the leaves and stick everything on the front of the card after the IRIS folding.

Card 2

Card: lily-white C110 (14.8 x 21 cm and 13.3 x 9 cm) • Pattern 6 • 2 cm wide strips from 4 different green envelopes • Green envelope paper (13.9 x 9.3 cm) • Gold holographic paper • Text sticker • Celestial corner scissors

Cut the corners off of the small card.

Card 3

Card: carnation white P03 (14.8 x 21 cm) and embossed champagne A2460 (13 x 8.5 cm) • Pattern 6 • 2 cm wide strips from 4 different green envelopes • Green envelope paper (13.8 x 9.5 cm) • Text sticker • Gold holographic paper • Multi-corner punch

Card 4

Card: white C335 (13 x 26 cm and 12 x 12.3 cm) and wine red P36 (12.5 x 12.8 cm) • Pattern 7 • 2 cm wide strips from 5 different envelopes • Green envelope paper (3 x 4 cm) • Gold holographic paper • Autumn embossing stencil • Exchangeable toadstool punch shape • Ridge master

Emboss the top and bottom of the smallest card. Cut out the cap and the stem of the mushroom separately. First, put a strip of envelope paper through the ridge master. Cut the bottom to the correct shape and stick it on the back of the card at the top of the stem. Cover the rest of the stem with envelope paper. Decorate the card with toadstools from the punch.

Card 5

Card: white C335 (13 x 26 cm and 12 x 12 cm) • Pattern 7 • 2 cm wide strips from 5 different pink envelopes • Pink envelope paper (3 x 4 cm) • Old rose envelope paper (12.3 x 12.3 cm) • Text sticker

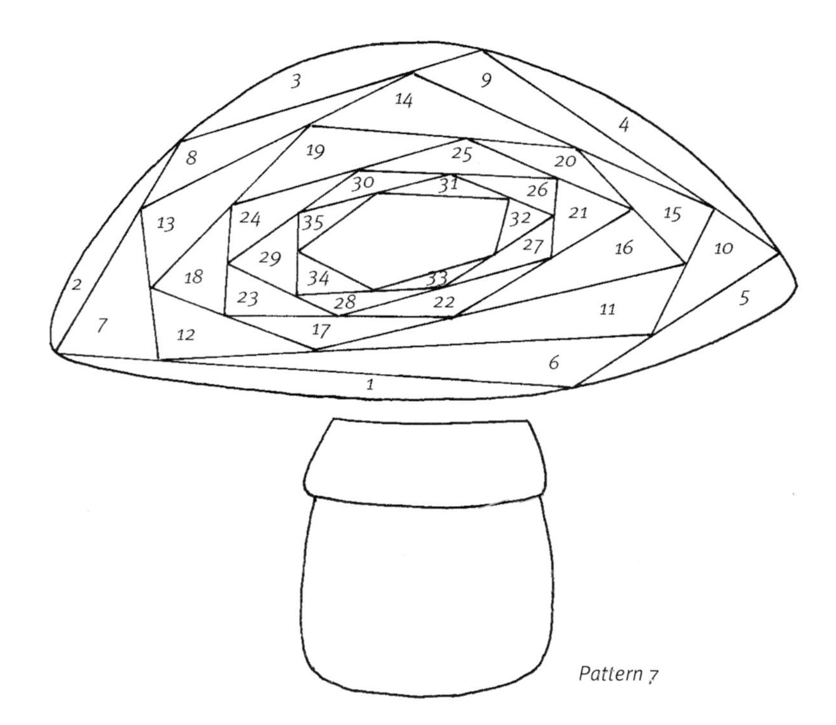

Pattern 7

• Silver deco tape • Exchangeable toadstool punch shape • Ridge master

Card 6

Card: white C335 (13 x 26 cm and 12 x 12 cm) • Pattern 7 • 2 cm wide strips from 5 different grey envelopes • Red envelope paper (12.4 x 12.4 cm) • Envelope paper (colour B) (3 x 4 cm) • Silver holographic paper • Victorian silhouette corner punch • Ridge master

Punch out the corners.

Card 7

Card: grey-pink C426 (13 x 26 cm) and mouse grey C345 (12 x 12 cm) • Pattern 7 • 2 cm wide strips from 5 different envelopes ranging in colour from white to brown • White envelope paper (3 x 4 cm) • Gold holographic paper • Text sticker • Fly corner punch • Ridge master

Punch out two corners.

Coffee time

Friends, drinking coffee and IRIS folding. An excellent combination.

All the cards are made according to the description given for card 1.

Card 1

Card: white A211 (13 x 26 cm and 11.7 x 10.5 cm) • Pattern 8 • 2 cm wide strips from 4 different red envelopes • Red envelope paper (12.5 x 11.8 cm) • Text sticker • Gold holographic paper • Flower corner punch

Punch out the top corners of the small card. After the IRIS folding, cut out the spout, lid and handle from envelope paper and stick them on the jug. Stick this on the sheet of red envelope paper and then on the double card.

Card 2

Card: white C335 (13 x 26 cm and 12 x 9.8 cm) • Model 8 • 2 cm wide strips from 4 different blue envelopes • Blue envelope paper (12.5 x 12.5 cm) • Text sticker • Gold deco tape • Drop ornamental border punch • Regal corner scissors

2.

4.

Round off the top corners of the small card. Decorate the sheet of blue envelope paper with four borders of drops.

Card 3

Card: white C335 (13 x 26 cm and 11.5 x 9.8 cm) • Model 8 • 2 cm wide strips from 4 different blue envelopes • Blue envelope paper (11.8 x 11.8 cm) • Text sticker • Silver deco tape • Regal corner scissors

Round off the top right hand corner and the bottom left hand corner of the small card using the corner scissors.

Card 4

Card: white C335 (13 x 26 cm and 11.5 x 11.5 cm) • Pattern 8 • 2 cm wide strips from 4 different aubergine, green and brown envelopes • Brown envelope paper (12 x 12 cm) • Text sticker • Gold holographic paper • Victorian embossing stencil

Emboss the corners of the small card.

3
4
8
12
7
16
11
20
15
24
28
19
32
29
25
23
21
17
27
31
30
13
26
22
9
18
5
14
2
6
10
1

Pattern 8

Cups

One or two, hanging or standing, you can never have enough cups.

Card 1

Card: dark red (14.8 x 21 cm) and light pink C103 (10.5 x 8 cm) • Pattern 9 • 2 cm wide strips from 4 different pink and red envelopes • Pink envelope paper (12.2 x 8.7 cm) • Text stickers • Copper deco tape

Only cut out the cup. After the IRIS folding, cut the handle out of envelope paper and stick it on the card with the text stickers.

Card 2

Card: royal blue C495 (14.8 x 21 cm) and white (13.8 x 9.8 cm) • Patterns 9 and 10 • 2 cm wide strips from 4 different blue envelopes • Text sticker • Silver deco tape • Regal corner scissors

Round off the top right-hand corner and the bottom left-hand corner.

Card 3

Card: white A211 (14.8 x 21 cm) and dark blue C500 (14.3 x 10 cm) • Pattern 10 • 2 cm wide strips from 4 different lilac/grey envelopes • Gold deco tape • Multi-corner punch • Split pins

Add the split pins after the IRIS folding, before sticking everything on the double card.

Card 4

Card: almond green C480 (14.8 x 21 cm and 11.5 x 9.3 cm) • Pattern 10 • 2 cm wide strips from 4 different envelopes • White envelope paper (14 x 9.9 cm) • Gold holographic paper • Drop ornamental border punch • Regal corner scissors

Round off the corners of the small card and the sheet of envelope paper. Punch out the drop border in the middle of the short sides of the sheet of envelope paper. After the IRIS folding, cut out a cup from the red envelope paper and make the bottom slant.

Card 5

Card: red C505 (14.8 x 21 cm and 11.9 x 8.4 cm) • Pattern 9 • 2 cm wide strips from 4 different cream and green envelopes • Cream envelope paper (13.5 x 8.9 cm) • Text sticker • Gold holographic paper • Cord ornamental border punch • Flower corner punch

Punch out the corners of the small card and use the border punch on the sheet of envelope paper.

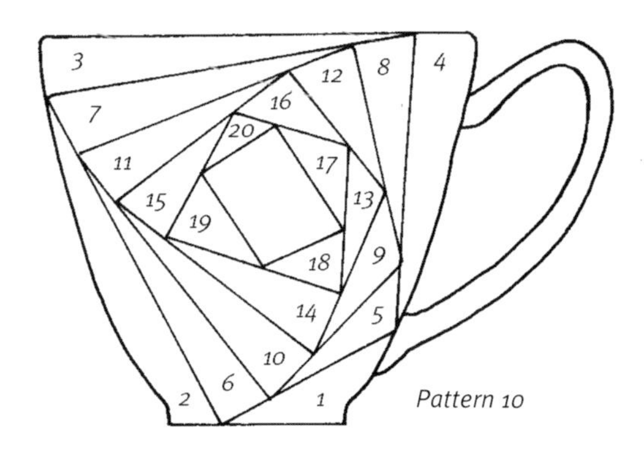

Pattern 10

Card 6

Card: wine red C503 (14.8 x 21 cm) and white C335 (14.2 x 9.8 cm) • Patterns 9 and 10 • 2 cm wide strips from 4 different pink/red envelopes • Pink envelope paper (14.6 x 10.2 cm) • Text sticker • Silver deco tape • Tulip corner punch

Punch out the corners of the white card.

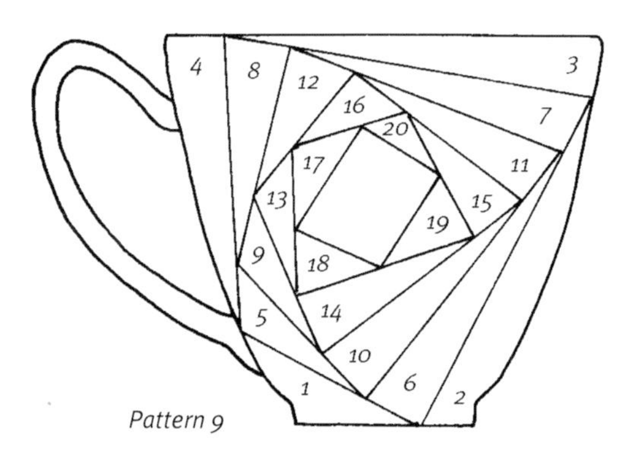

Pattern 9

Card 7

Card: indigo blue C140 (10.5 x 29.7 cm) and white (9.8 x 14 cm) • Pattern 9 • 2 cm wide strips from 4 different blue envelopes • Gold deco tape • Multi-corner punch • Split pins

Punch out two corners of the white card.

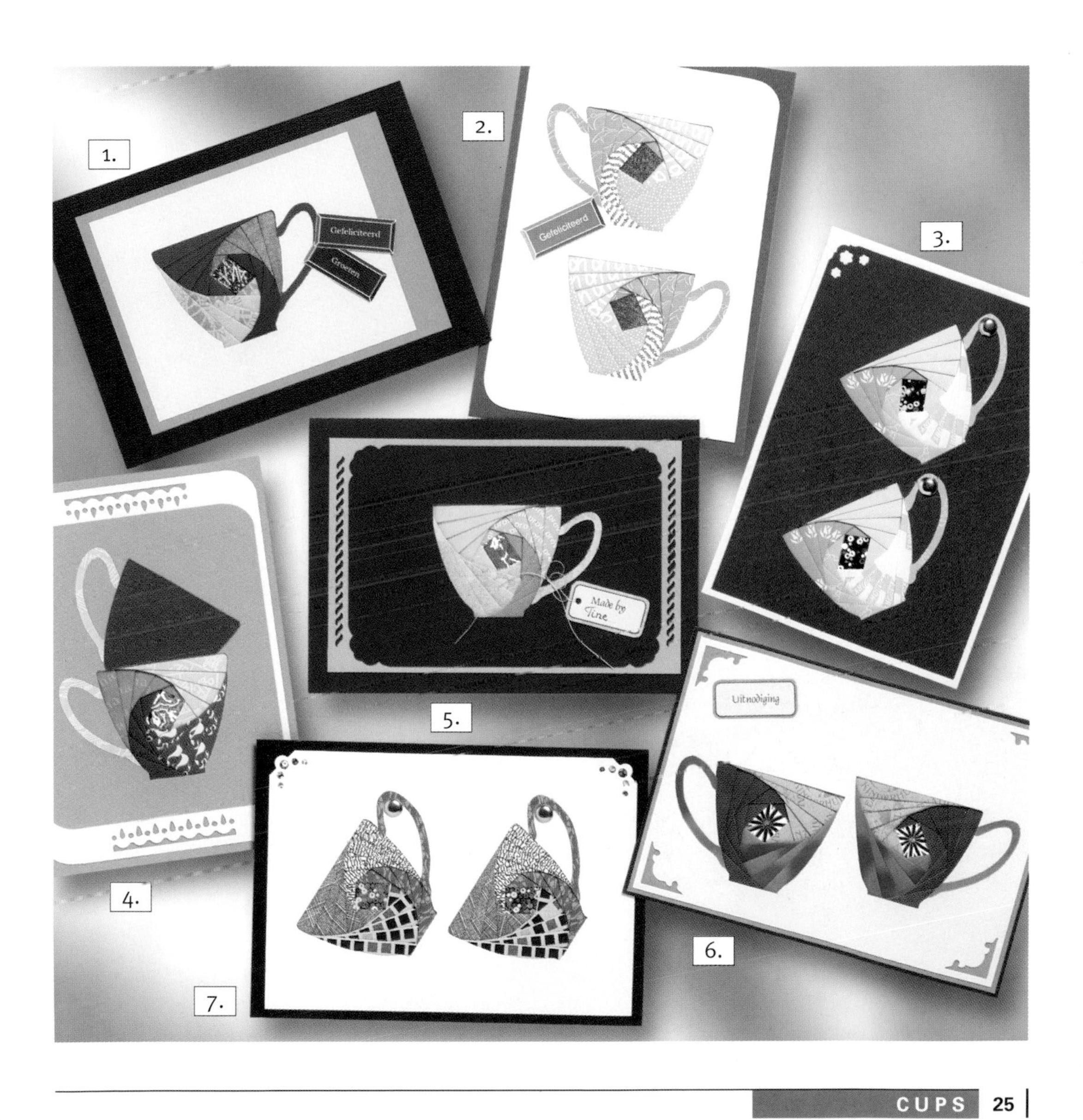
1.
2.
3.
4.
5.
6.
7.
Gefeliciteerd
Groeten
Gefeliciteerd
Made by Tine
Uitnodiging

Lanterns and icicles

Light and glistening

in the winter.

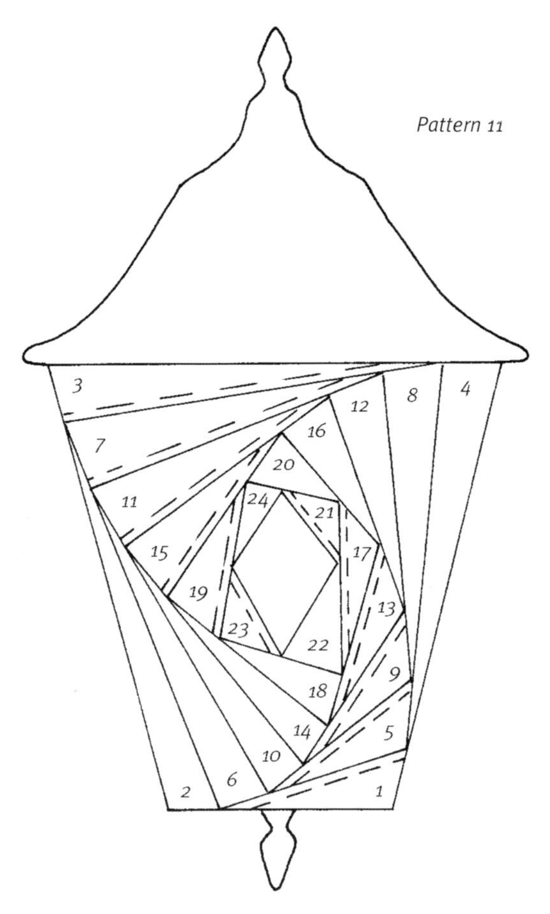

The lanterns are made according to the description given for the card on the cover of this book. The icicles are made according to the description given for card 4.

Card on the cover

Card: white C335 (14.8 x 21 cm and 13.7 x 9.5 cm) • Pattern 11 • 2 cm wide strips from 4 different purple envelopes • Aubergine envelope paper (14.2 x 9.9 cm) • Purple envelope paper (5 x 7 cm) • Gold holographic paper for the middle of the card and 1 cm wide glitter strips • Multi-corner punch

Punch out the top corners and cut the part of the lantern which will be iris folded out of the small white card. See Techniques for instructions on how to use the glitter strips. Cut the lid and the point out of the purple paper and the rays of light out of the gold holographic paper.

Card 1

Card: ivory white C111 (14.8 x 21 cm) and Christmas red P43 (14 x 9.6 cm) • Pattern 11 • 2 cm wide strips from 4 different beige envelopes • Beige envelope paper (5 x 7 cm) • Text sticker • Gold holographic paper for the middle of the card

and 1 cm wide glitter strips • Holly corner punch
Punch out the top corners of the red card.

Card 2

Card: cerise P33 (14.8 x 21 cm), ivory white C111 (13.5 x 8.6 cm) and gold (14 x 9 cm) • Pattern 11 • 2 cm wide strips from 4 different red envelopes • Red envelope paper (5 x 7 cm) • Text sticker • Gold holographic paper for the middle of the card and 1 cm wide glitter strips • Star corner punch
Punch out the top corners of the white card.

Card 3

Card: white (14.8 x 21 cm) and indigo blue C140 (13.8 x 9.5) • Pattern 11 • 2 cm wide strips from 3 different grey envelopes • 2 cm wide strips of silver holographic paper for sections 1, 5, 9, etc. • Grey envelope paper (5 x 7 cm) • Text sticker • Silver holographic paper • Multi-corner punch
Punch out the top corners of the blue card.

Card 4

*Card: white C335 (14.8 x 21 cm and 11.8 x 8.5 cm) • Pattern 12 • 2 cm wide strips from 4 different purple envelopes • Purple envelope paper (14x9 cm) * Gold deco tape • Star chain ornamental border punch*
Punch out the border of the sheet of envelope paper. Cut 1 cm wide strips from the deco tape and add them to colours B and D as glitter strips.

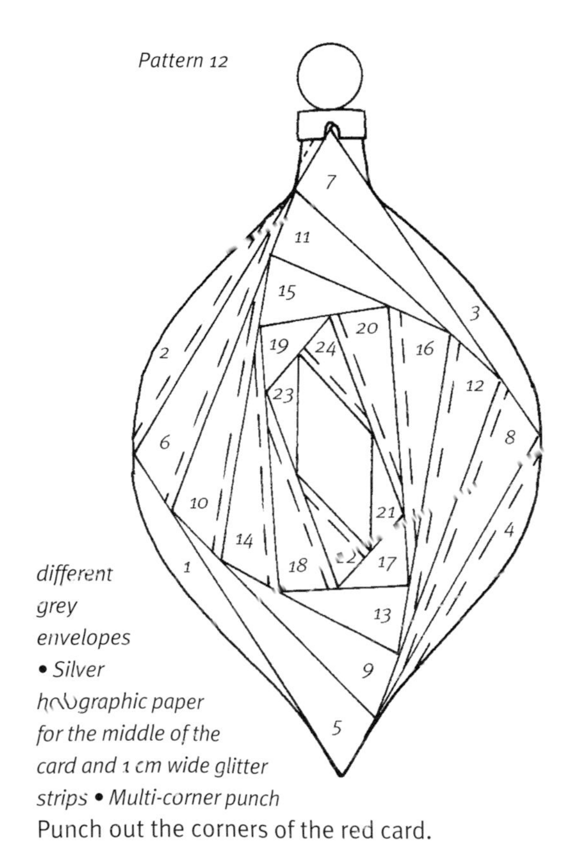
Pattern 12

Card 5

Card: lavender P21 (14.8 x 21 cm) and burgundy (13.8 x 9.5 cm) • Pattern 12 • 2 cm wide strips from 4 different grey envelopes • Silver holographic paper for the middle of the card and 1 cm wide glitter strips • Multi-corner punch
Punch out the corners of the red card.

Card 6

Card: purple P46 (14.8 x 21 cm) and white C335 (13.5 x 9.5 cm) • Pattern 12 • 2 cm wide strips from 4 different red and purple envelopes • Silver holographic paper for the middle of the card and 1 cm wide glitter strips • Star corner punch
Punch out the corners of the white card.

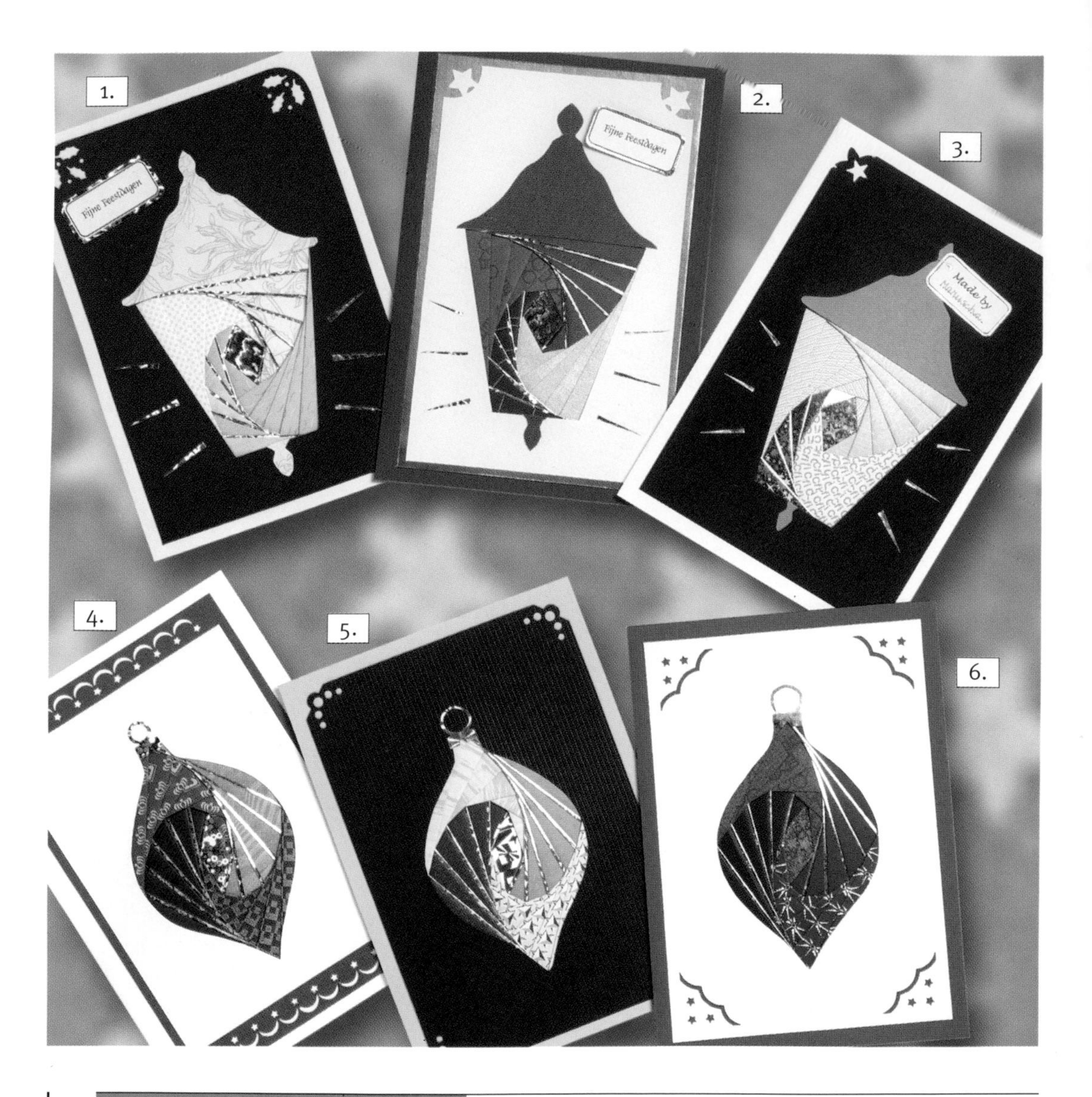
1.
2.
3.
4.
5.
6.
Fijne Feestdagen
Fijne Feestdagen
Made by

1.
Fijne Feestdagen
2.
3.
Fijne Feestdagen
5.
Fijne Feestdagen
4.
Fijne Feestdagen
6.
7.

Christmas hut and tree

Stylish and dignified. Attractive in Christmas red, purple and blue with silver or gold.

Card 1

Card: Christmas red P43 (13 x 26 cm), white C335 (7.5 x 6.5 cm) and silver (8 x 7 cm) • Pattern 13 • 2 cm wide strips of silver and red origami paper and silver holographic paper • Christmas white vellum (13 x 26 cm) with a 8.5 x 7.5 cm window • Silver deco tape • Text sticker • Star chain ornamental border punch

Cut the hut out of the white card. After the IRIS folding, stick the eye on top of the hut and the punched out small stars around it. Stick the text sticker on the red card.

Card 2

Card: white C335 (13 x 26 cm and 11.5 x 11.5 cm) and silver holographic (11.9 x 11.9 cm) • Pattern 14 • 2 cm wide strips from 3 different cerise and grey envelopes • Red envelope paper (12.2 x 12.2 cm) • Text sticker • Silver holographic paper

Cut the tree out of the small white card. Cut the right-hand side of the white card at an angle, remaining at least 0.5 cm from the tree. Cut the holographic card and the red envelope paper, each time, 0.2 cm wider than the card above it.

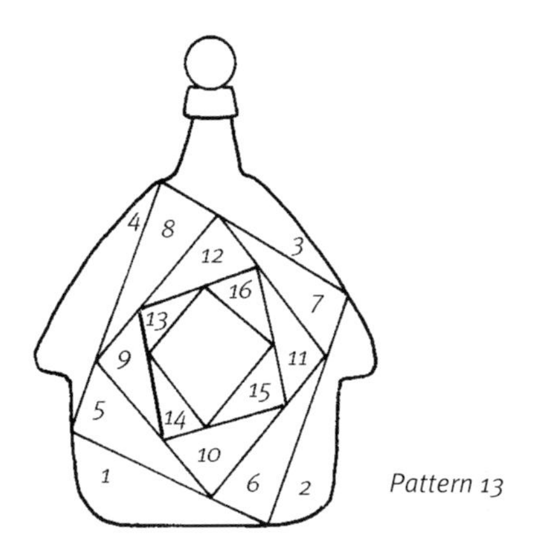

Pattern 13

Card 3

Card: white C335 (14.8 x 21 cm and 12.3 x 9.2 cm) • Pattern 14 • 2 cm wide strips from 3 different purple envelopes • Purple envelope paper (13.5 x 9.5 cm) • Gold origami paper for the middle of the card and 1 cm wide glitter strips • Regal corner scissors • Multi-corner punch

Round off the top corners of the small card.

Card 4

Card: white C335 (14.8 x 21 cm and 12.6 x 9.3 cm) • Pattern 14 • 2 cm wide strips from 3 different blue envelopes • Blue envelope paper (14 x 9.6 cm) • Text sticker • Silver holographic paper • Star punch • Celestial corner scissors

Cut off the top corners of the small card using the corner scissors.

Card 5 (on the cover)

Card: wine red P36 (13 x 26 cm), white C335 (12.2 x 11 cm) and gold (12.9 x 11.5 cm) • Pattern 14 • 2 cm wide strips from 3 different purple/wine red envelopes • Text sticker • Gold holographic paper • Multi-corner punch

Make this card according to the description given for card 2.

Card 6

Card: purple P46 (13 x 26 cm), white C335 (7.5 x 6.5 cm) and gold (8 x 7 cm) • Pattern 13 • 2 cm wide strips of gold holographic paper and gold and purple origami paper • Christmas white vellum (13 x 26 cm) with a 8.5 x 7.5 cm window

Make this card according to the description given for card 1.

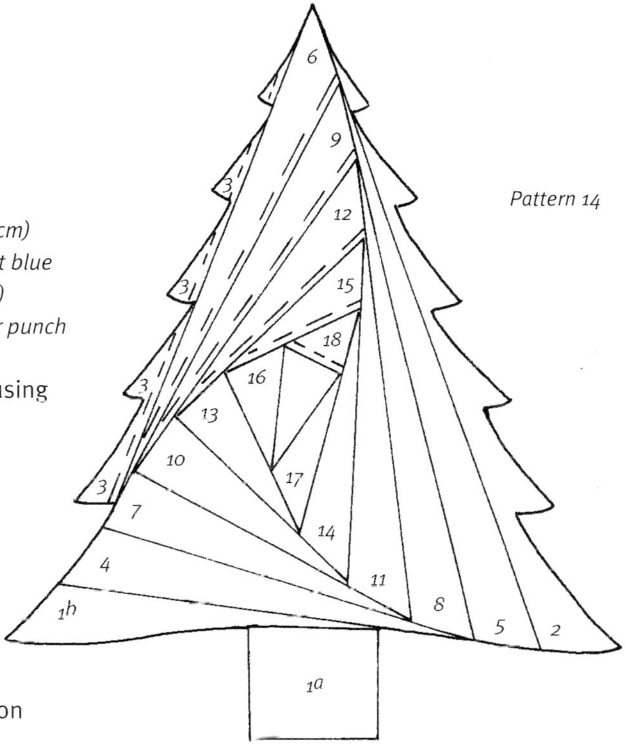

Pattern 14

Card 7

Card: white (13 x 26 cm and 11.8 x 9.5 cm) • Pattern 14 • 2 cm wide strips from 3 different purple-blue envelopes • Purple envelope paper (12.2 x 12.4 cm) • Text sticker • Gold origami paper for the middle of the card and 1 cm wide glitter strips • Star chain ornamental border punch

Use the ornamental border punch on the sheet of envelope paper, using the last punched star as the starting point for the next link in the chain.

Pattern 6

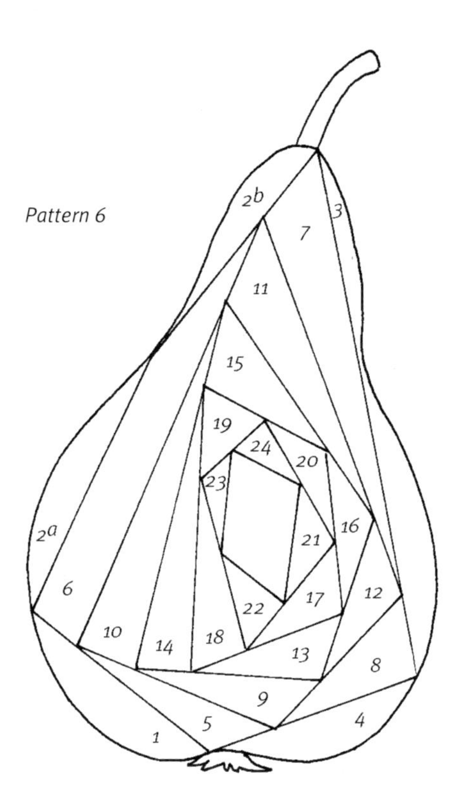

Thanks to:
Kars & Co B.V., Ochten,
the Netherlands and
Koninklijke Talens, Apeldoorn,
the Netherlands (for the card material)

The materials used can be ordered by shopkeepers from:
your wholesaler/supplier